A NOTE TO PARENTS

When your children are ready to "step into reading," giving them the right books—and lots of them—is as crucial as giving them the right food to eat. **Step into Reading Books** present exciting stories and information reinforced with lively, colorful illustrations that make learning to read fun, satisfying, and worthwhile. They are priced so that acquiring an entire library of them is affordable. And they are beginning readers with an important difference—they're written on four levels.

Step 1 Books, with their very large type and extremely simple vocabulary, have been created for the very youngest readers. **Step 2 Books** are both longer and slightly more difficult. **Step 3 Books,** written to mid-second-grade reading levels, are for the child who has acquired even greater reading skills. **Step 4 Books** offer exciting nonfiction for the increasingly proficient reader.

Children develop at different ages. **Step into Reading Books,** with their four levels of reading, are designed to help children become good—and interested—readers *faster.* The grade levels assigned to the four steps—preschool through grade 1 for Step 1, grades 1 through 3 for Step 2, grades 2 and 3 for Step 3, and grades 2 through 4 for Step 4—are intended only as guides. Some children move through all four steps very rapidly; others climb the steps over a period of several years. These books will help your child "step into reading" in style!

To Jaya
—L.R.P.

With thanks to
Dr. Glenn Storrs
of the Yale-
Peabody Museum.

Text copyright © 1991 by Lucille Recht Penner. Illustrations copyright © 1991 by Peter Barrett. All rights reserved under International and Pan-American Copyright Conventions. Published in the United States by Random House, Inc., New York, and simultaneously in Canada by Random House of Canada Limited, Toronto.

Library of Congress Cataloging-in-Publication Data
Penner, Lucille Recht. Dinosaur babies / by Lucille Recht Penner.   p.   cm. — (Step into reading. A Step 1 book) Summary: Describes the characteristics and behavior of baby dinosaurs. ISBN 0-679-81207-5 (trade)— ISBN 0-679-91207-X (lib. bdg.) 1. Dinosaurs—Infancy—Juvenile literature. [1. Dinosaurs—Infancy.]   I. Title. II. Series: Step into reading. Step 1 book. QE862.D5P45 1991   90-36045   567.9′1–dc20

Manufactured in the United States of America   21 22 23 24 25 26 27 28 29 30

STEP INTO READING is a trademark of Random House, Inc.

Step into Reading

DINOSAUR BABIES

By Lucille Recht Penner

Illustrated by Peter Barrett

A Step 1 Book

Random House 🏠 New York

Squeak! Squeak!
Is that the sound
of a baby dinosaur
calling to its mother?

Apatosaurus
(a-PAT-uh-sor-us)

Nobody knows.

Nobody has ever heard
a baby dinosaur.

Nobody has seen one.

All the dinosaurs died
millions of years ago.
But we know a lot
about them from what
dinosaur hunters have
found...

footprints

teeth

bones

They have found small
baby bones in nests.

They have even found
dinosaur eggs.
Most dinosaurs were very big.
But their eggs were small.

The smallest was only
as big as a quarter.

The biggest was about
the size of a football!

Were dinosaurs good mothers?
This kind of dinosaur was.
She made a nest of mud
and laid her eggs in it.
Chickens sit on their eggs.

Maiasaura
(my-uh-SOR-uh)

But this dinosaur did not.

She was too heavy.

The eggs would break!

She put leaves on the eggs

to keep them warm.

The mother watched the nest.
Lots of animals liked to eat
dinosaur eggs!
She kept them away.

Inside the eggs
the babies grew.
They breathed through
tiny holes in the eggshells.

Troödon
(TRO-o-don)

One day the eggs cracked!

Little baby dinosaurs came out.

They were hungry.

Maybe they squeaked.

The mother dinosaur
brought them food.
The babies ate and ate
all day long.

Dinosaur babies
had big heads and big eyes.
They could see and hear well.

Psittacosaurus
(SIT-uh-ko-SOR-us)

Tyrannosaurus
(tie-RAN-uh-SOR-us)

Human babies are born
without any teeth.
Not dinosaur babies!
They had lots of teeth.

Apatosaurus
(a-PAT-uh-sor-us)

What did baby dinosaurs eat?
Some kinds ate leaves and
berries and seeds.

Some kinds ate little animals
and bugs.

Deinonychus
(die-NON-ee-kus)

Was it safe for baby dinosaurs to hunt for food alone? No! Enemies were all around. And baby dinosaurs could not fight or run fast. They could only hide.

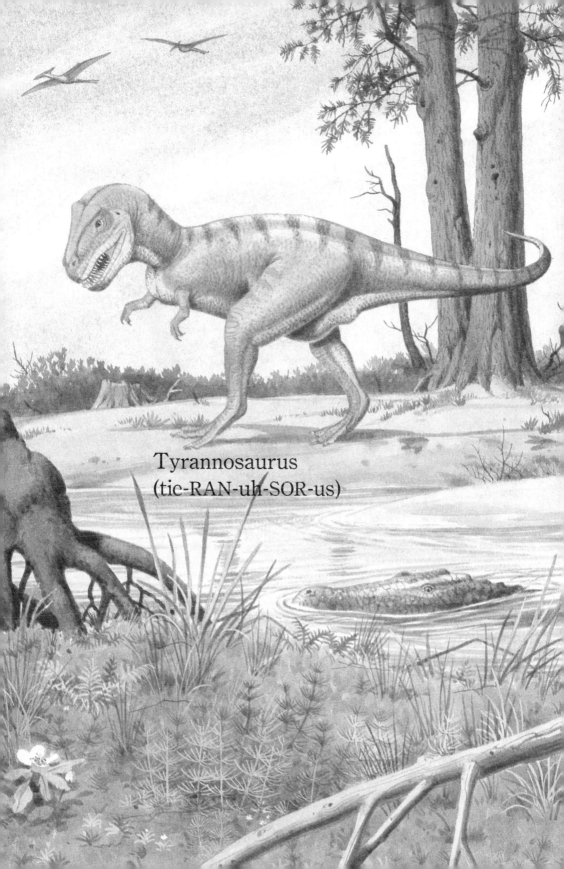

Tyrannosaurus
(tic-RAN-uh-SOR-us)

Some baby dinosaurs
were lucky.

Triceratops
(try-SER-uh-tops)

They were never alone.
They lived in herds.

Even then enemies

tried to grab

the babies and eat them!

So the dinosaurs made a circle.

Little ones stayed on the inside.

Big ones guarded the outside.

Babies were safe

in the dinosaur herd.

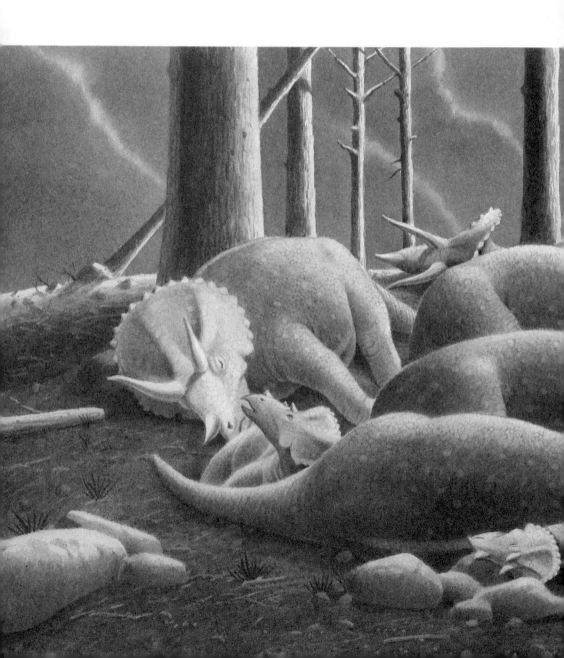

The dinosaurs walked and ate
and slept together.

Baby dinosaurs kept growing and changing.

Styracosaurus
(sty-RAK-uh-SOR-us)

Some kinds grew sharp horns.

Some kinds grew spikes on their tails.

Stegosaurus
(STEG-uh-SOR-us)

Others grew bony frills.

Protoceratops
(PRO-tuh-SER-uh-tops)

Brachiosaurus
(BRAY-kee-uh-SOR-us)

They grew until
they weren't babies
anymore.
Some grew to be the
biggest animals ever
to walk the earth!

And some had
dinosaur babies
of their own.